HOW TO DRAW
FLOWERS
AND
PLANTS

Mark Bergin

BOOK HOUSE

SALARIYA

Published in Great Britain in MMXIII by
Book House, an imprint of
The Salariya Book Company Ltd
25 Marlborough Place, Brighton BN1 1UB

3 5 7 9 8 6 4 2

Author: **Mark Bergin** was born in Hastings in 1961. He studied at Eastbourne College of Art and has specialised in historical reconstructions as well as aviation and maritime subjects since 1983. He lives in Bexhill-on-Sea with his wife and three children.

Editor: Rob Walker

PB ISBN: 978-1-908973-75-7

A CIP catalogue record for this book is available from the British Library.

Printed and bound in China.
Printed on paper from sustainable sources.
Reprinted in MMXIII.

WARNING: Fixatives should be used only under adult supervision.

Visit our websites to read interactive **free** web books, stay up to date with new releases, catch up with us on the Book House Blog, view our electronic catalogue and more!

www.salariya.com
Free electronic versions of four of our *You Wouldn't Want to Be* titles

www.book-house.co.uk
Online catalogue
Information books
and graphic novels

www.scribobooks.com
Fiction books

www.scribblersbooks.com
Books for babies, toddlers and pre-school children

**www.flickr.com/photos/
salariyabookhouse**
View our photostream with sneak previews of forthcoming titles

Join the conversation on Facebook and Twitter by visiting
www.salariya.com

Visit
www.salariya.com
for our online catalogue and
free interactive web books.

PAPER FROM
SUSTAINABLE
FORESTS

Contents

4 Making a start

6 Drawing materials

8 Ways of looking

10 Choosing a theme

12 Composition

14 Light and tone

16 Using photos

18 2D flowers

20 Sunflowers

22 Roses

24 Daffodils

26 Chrysanthemums

28 Thistle

30 Hibiscus

32 Glossary and Index

Making a start

The first stage of drawing flowers is to choose your flower and then decide which medium you want to use to depict it. You can draw flowers as found objects in their natural setting or in artificial groupings.

Drawing construction lines to outline petals and leaves will help guide you when drawing flowers, as shown above.

'Artificial' subjects are made when the artist purposely arranges a group of flowers against a backdrop.

'Found' objects are things that catch your eye — such as flowers in a garden setting — and are drawn just as they are.

Sketch simple flower constructions.

Detailed observation of a delphinium.

4

Saffron crocus in ink.

Practise sketching house plants and flowers around your home.

Sketching everyday objects will help you understand the perspective all around you.

The only way to get better is to keep practising. If a drawing looks wrong, start again. Keep working at it.

5

Drawing materials

There are many different ways to approach a drawing. Try different materials such as pencils, pen and ink, brush pens, felt—tip pens and coloured pencils. Each creates a quite different result that will add variety to your drawings.

Wood anemone silhouette.

Felt—tips come in a range of line widths. The broader tips are good for filling in large areas of flat tone.

Lines drawn in **ink** cannot be erased, so keep ink drawings sketchy and less precise. Don't worry about mistakes as they can be lost in the linework as the drawing develops.

Sketch of foxgloves using a graphic ink pen.

6

Hard pencils are more grey; soft pencils are blacker. Hard pencils are graded from 6H (the hardest) through 5H, 4H, 3H, 2H and H.

Soft pencils are graded from B, 2B, 3B, 4B and 5B up to 6B (the softest).

It can be tricky adding light and shade with an ink pen. Analyse your drawing. The lightest areas should be left untouched. Then apply solid areas of ink to the darkest parts. The midtones are achieved by hatching (single parallel lines) or cross–hatching (criss–crossed lines).

Felt–pen drawing of a common poppy.

7

Ways of looking

There are different ways of drawing a flower composition, from a realistic approach to abstract forms.

Try varying the amount of detail in your drawing. The more detailed, the more realistic the result. The more sketchy, the more impressionistic your composition will be.

Pencil study of a rose.

Floral study in felt—tip pen

Drawing only the outline of each shape can create
a more abstract composition. Look carefully at
the spaces between objects — artists call this
'negative space'.

Working in line with some solid
blocks of shading, rather than using
a tonal approach, can make your
drawing very striking.

Ink-pen study using
heavy black tone.

9

Choosing a theme

The choice of theme is endless and down to individual tastes. It can range from traditional flower arrangements and bouquets to simple garden flowers. Choose whatever inspires you.

Think of a theme you would like to draw and collect the objects you need; or just find suitable flowers in their natural environment.

Coloured—pencil sketch of flowers in a container.

Hydrangeas and ribbons drawn in ink.

Roses in a china vase.

Sketching garden or wild flowers in their original habitat can add interest to your drawings.

Making up your own floral arrangements to sketch gives you greater control over composition and lighting conditions.

The sinuous shapes of bindweed make it an interesting subject to sketch. You often find it in gardens or hedges.

Composition

Composition is the arrangement of the parts of your drawing on the surface of the paper. Even when you're only drawing a single flower, consider whether it will look best in the centre of the paper or off centre.

The composition of this drawing is based on the golden rectangle. Ever since the ancient Greeks, artists have been fascinated by this graceful proportion.

1. Draw a square.

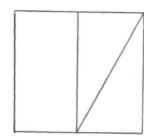

2. Divide it in half. In one half, draw a diagonal.

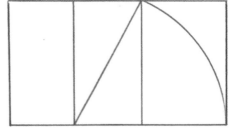

3. Setting your compasses on the ends of the diagonal, draw a curve as shown. This gives the length of your golden rectangle.

A composition based on the golden rectangle. Note how the main flower aligns with the edge of the original square.

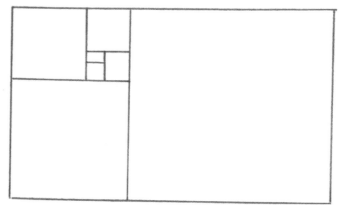

If you remove a square from your golden rectangle, the part left over is also a golden rectangle. You can keep on doing this as many times as you like.

This composition showcases a single plant.

In this composition, simplified flower shapes are carefully arranged to make an all-over pattern.

Subtle differences in the angle of the petals and the curve of the stems add life to this row of nearly identical blooms.

A close—up view of petals can give a completely different impression of a flower.

13

Light and tone

The way light hits an object plays a major role in the outcome of your drawing. It is well worth taking time to consider the direction and strength of your light source.

In this view the light comes from above and casts a shadow below.

This time the light comes from the front and casts a shadow behind the vase.

Light source

Light source

Light source

The light here is coming from the left, so it casts a shadow to the right.

Adding a dark background tone makes the vase and flowers stand out.

A dark background throws the flowers into relief.

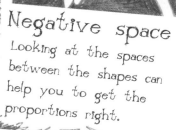

Negative space

Looking at the spaces between the shapes can help you to get the proportions right.

In this ink sketch, dark tones in the foliage make the flowers stand out.

Using photos

Drawing flowers from photographs can help you to identify shape and form, and will train you to draw accurately.

First choose a good photograph of flowers and trace it. Then draw a grid of squares over the tracing.

Now draw a faint grid of the same proportions onto your drawing paper. Copy the shapes within each square of the tracing paper onto the grid of your drawing paper.

When drawing, remember to keep your viewpoint constant — moving about will change your point of view!

Light source

Once the outline shape is complete, add more details to the drawing. Always refer back to the grid for accuracy.

To add form to your drawing, see where the light falls, and add shadows to the parts that face away from the light.

Add tone to the flowers, the background and the foreground.

Give the vase a three-dimensional shape by using hatching and cross-hatching.

17

2D Flowers

T wo—dimensional flower shapes, whether realistic or simplified, really lend themselves to creating interesting designs and patterns.

If an object has a very distinctive shape it may need very little visual information to describe it.

Flattened drawings of flower shapes.

Use your imagination and create your own flower designs using this type of flat drawing technique.

Simple outline drawing of grass and flowers.

Use a dark background to make the flower shapes stand out.

Try filling a whole page with repeating patterns. They needn't always repeat exactly.

Felt pens are useful when drawing two—dimensional flowers because they allow you to block in large areas of flat colour quickly.

19

Sunflowers

The sunflower is so named because its huge head and fringe of yellow petals are often said to look like the sun.

Begin by drawing three circles, as shown, one inside the other.

Draw in a line for the sunflower stalk.

Try to keep a light touch with these construction lines, as you may wish to erase some of them later.

Add another line to thicken the stalk. Draw in big leaves using sweeping pencil strokes.

In the outer ring draw tiny circles to represent the seeds. The seeds in the centre are more tightly packed (see detail below).

Composition

Try framing your drawing with a rectangle or a square – this can make the composition look completely different.

Draw in the petals. Layer them behind each other to create a feeling of depth.

Now begin to add detail to the leaves.

Adding darker shading where the light would not reach will make your drawing more realistic.

Use shading and tone to add the final details to the flower.

A sunflower head in close–up makes a fascinating study by itself. The tiny flowers in the centre (which later become seeds) are arranged in interlocking spirals.

Remove any unwanted construction lines.

Roses

oses are widely grown for their beauty and fragrance. Indeed, they are ancient symbols of love and beauty. The rose is the national flower of England.

Draw a large oval with a smaller one inside. Add a line passing through the centre for the stem.

The middle of the rose must be drawn with the petals closely clustered together.

Using a mirror

Try looking at your drawing in a mirror. Seeing it in reverse can help you spot mistakes.

Sketch in the
outermost petals.

Add more petals,
spacing them
further apart.

Make the stem
thicker and draw
in the leaves.

Adding darker shading
to the side that
faces away from the
light will make your
drawing more realistic.

Use shading and tone to
add texture to the
surface of the petals.

Add detail to the
leaves. Give them
jagged edges and veins.

Remove any unwanted
construction lines.

Add thorns to
the stem.

23

Daffodils

Daffodils have a unique trumpet—shaped flower and are a cheerful yellow colour. The daffodil is the national flower of Wales, where it is traditional to wear one on St David's Day.

Start by drawing two circles and two ovals, as shown.

Draw the stems, one straight, one bent.

Use these shapes as guides to sketch in the petals.

Add the trumpet shape.

As this flower is viewed from the side, the petals appear narrower because of foreshortening.

Thicken the stems and add long, curved leaves.

Draw an unopened flowerhead behind the other two flowers.

Begin adding detail to the flowerheads and leaves.

Remove any unwanted construction lines.

Add shading to the darkest areas to give greater depth to your drawing.

25

Chrysanthemums

Chrysanthemums come in many colours, shapes and varieties. The flowerheads are formed from densely packed petals.

Start by drawing two large ovals. Then draw two smaller ovals inside them.

Draw in two lines for the stalks.

Remember to draw these construction lines lightly so they can easily be erased later.

Add a bud shape in between the two large flowerheads.

Add a second line to show the thickness of the stems.

Draw in the tightly packed petals of the opening bud.

Working from the centre outwards, continue to draw all the petals of the chrysanthemum.

Start drawing in the petal shapes.

Sketch in jagged leaves on the stems.

Complete the drawing using a soft coloured pencil. This can be blurred easily to vary the shading of your drawing.

Remove any unwanted construction lines.

Add the darkest areas of tone to parts that face away from the light.

Thistle

The thistle is the national emblem of Scotland. It is a very prickly flower, but its distinctive shape is rewarding to draw.

Draw ovals for the flowerheads.

Add flowing lines for the flower stems.

Add detail to the lower half of each oval. Then draw in the fan—like outline of the petals on top.

Thicken the stem lines.

Add detail to the flowerheads.

Draw in the leaves. Use jagged lines to make them look spiky.

Add veins to the centre line of each leaf.

Complete the final details, adding shading and toning to give a three-dimensional effect.

The thistle's head is densely packed with spikes. Draw many short lines to represent these.

Add thorns to the stems.

Remove any unwanted construction lines.

29

Hibiscus

Hibiscus plants have large, colourful trumpet—shaped flowers. These come in many colours, including yellow, pink, red, white, purple and orange.

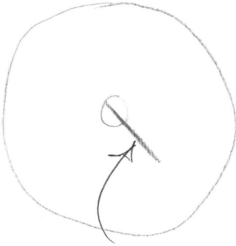

Draw a large circle wth a smaller one inside it. Draw a line out from the centre.

Keep all construction lines faint so they can be easily erased.

Add a small star to the end of the line. This will become the stamens.

Sketch in five large petals, using your outer circle as a guide.

Start adding details to the petals using small lines.

Add shading to the flower centre to create a feeling of depth.

Add little circles to the ends of the stamens.

Draw in some smaller leaves behind the flower.

Begin drawing in the leaves surrounding the flower.

Add veins to the centre line of each leaf.

Add shading to the petals, stamens and leaves. This will give your finished drawing a three—dimensional effect.

This detail of the stamens shows the pollen carried on their ends.

Add the darkest areas of tone where light wouldn't reach.

Remove any unwanted construction lines.

Glossary

Composition The arrangement of the various parts of a picture on the drawing paper.

Construction lines Guidelines used in the early stages of a drawing; they are usually erased later.

Cross—hatching A series of criss—cross lines used to add dense shade to a drawing.

Foreshortening Drawing part of an object shorter or narrower than it would usually appear, to give the impression that it is angled towards or away from the viewer.

Found composition A composition in which objects are shown just as the artist found them, rather than being deliberately arranged by the artist.

Hatching A series of parallel lines used to add shade to a drawing.

Light source The direction from which the light seems to come in a drawing.

Negative space The empty space left between the parts of a drawing. It can be an important part of the composition in itself.

Silhouette A drawing that shows only a solid dark shape, like a shadow.

Stamens The organs inside a flower that produce pollen.

Three—dimensional Having an effect of depth, so as to look lifelike or real.

Index

A
artificial subjects 4

C
chrysanthemum 26—27
close—up details 13, 21, 31
coloured pencils 10
composition 12—13, 21
construction lines 4
cross—hatching 7, 17

D
daffodil 24—25

F
felt—tips 6, 7, 8
found subjects 4

G
golden rectangle 12
grids 16

H
hatching 7, 17
hibiscus 30—31

L
light source 14

M
materials 6—7
mirror 22

N
negative space 9, 15

O
outline drawing 9

P
pencils 7, 8, 10
pens 5, 6, 7, 9,
photographs 16—17

R
repeating patterns 13, 19
rose 22—23

S
shading 7, 9, 14—15
sketching 5, 11
stamens 31
sunflower 20—21

T
themes 10—11
thistle 28—29